NUGGETS

NUGGETS FROM MY POCKET

RITA KROON

A Walk to the Well

Nuggets from My Pocket
All Rights Reserved
Copyright © 2020 2023 Rita Kroon

Cover design

A Walk to the Well
www.awalktothewell.com

ISBN: 9780989198592

Printed on acid-free paper in the United States of America.

Acknowledgements

It is with a heart full of love for my husband, Burt, that I say thank you for your willingness to listen as I read. Your patience and tenderness encouraged me to persevere even when the words were difficult to find.

It is with deep gratitude to my daughter, LaDawn, for the many hours of technical expertise she spent in making this book possible. Thank you so much, LaDawn!

It is with much appreciation for my daughter, Rene', for her great insight and suggestions on the contents to make this book complete. Thank you so much, Rene'!

I cannot omit my daughter in Iowa for cheering me on over the phone. Thanks so much, Shelly, for being a major part of this team!

I am so grateful to my Lord and Savior for His indisputable Word, and to all those who left nuggets of His truth for us to glean.

Special Dedication

My current works are in loving memory of my husband, Burt, and our daughter, Rene', each of whom we shared our faith in our Lord Jesus Christ.

Rita Kroon

My Prayer

Heavenly Father, You are the God of grace and mercy and there is no other God besides You. Bless those of us who read these nuggets that we would take to heart Your message to each one of us. Grant that we may hear what is on Your heart so that we would delight in You and draw near to You and You would draw near to us. Grant us a deeper faith in Jesus Christ. May our hearts be filled with Your peace that surpasses all understanding and joy overflowing. In Jesus' matchless name, I ask.

Contents

Nuggets of . . .

Nuggets of . . .

Good and Better

It is *good to* know the promises of the Lord;
it is *better to* believe them.

~~~

It is *good to* trust God's love for you;
it is *better to* respond with love for Him.

~~~

It is *good to* have thankfulness
in all circumstances;
it is *better to* have deep joy
in the Holy Spirit.

~~~

It is *good to* be confident;
it is *better to* be eternally secure.

~~~

It is *good to* know the Scriptures;
it is *better to* know the power of God.

~~~

It is *good to* watch for Jesus' return;
it is *better to* watch with anticipation.

~~~

It *is good to* express love for Jesus;
it is *better to* be extravagant about it.

~~~

It is *good to* see God in all circumstances;
it is *better to* bless Him at all times.

~~~

It is *good to* see the beauty in the world;
it is *better to* gaze on the
beauty of the Creator.

~~~

It is *good to* have life;
it is *better to* have abundant life.

~~~

It is *good to* read God's Word;
it is *better to* live it.

~~~

It is *good to* trust God;
it is *better to* trust that God
will carry you through.

~~~

It is *good to* know God;
it is *better to* love, worship and obey God.

~~~

It is *good to* be available for God's purposes;
it is *better to* be intentional about it.

~~~

It is *good to* have faith;
it is *better to* put faith in action.

~~~

It is *good to* witness to and pray for others;
it is *better to* do so for those who do not listen.

~~~

It is *good to* be purified with fire;
it is *better to* come forth purified in faith.

~~~

It is *good to* know happiness in life;
it is *better to* know joy in the Lord.

~~~

It is *good to* know of God;
it is *better to* believe in God.

~~~

It is *good to* be convicted of sin;
it is *better to* be forgiven of sin.

~~~

It is *good to* serve the Lord;
it is *better to* serve the Lord with gladness.

~~~

It is *good to* love all people;
it is *better to* love people as God does.

~~~

It is *good to* have hope;
it is *better to* have hope in Jesus.

~~~

It is *good to* be confident;
it is *better* to be eternally secure.

~~~

It is *good to* know who you are as a person;
it is *better to* know who you are in God.

~~~

It is *good to* have spiritual gifts;
it is *better to* be faithful stewards
of spiritual gifts.

~~~

It is *good to* pray for another;
it is *better to* show love that adds
strength to prayer.

~~~

It is *good to* pray;
it is *better to* persevere in prayer.

~~~

It is good to be amazed at God;
it is better to be in awe of God.

~~~

Nuggets of . . .
Better Than

It is *better to* praise a spouse
than to stifle a spouse.

~~~

It is *better to* seek Jesus
than to find Satan.

~~~

It is *better to* have godly repentance
than to have worldly remorse.

~~~

It is *better to* encourage
than to criticize.

~~~

It is *better to* bless
than to blame.

~~~

It is *better to* rejoice
than to resent.

~~~

It is *better to* build bridges
than to build walls.

~~~

It is *better to* know Jesus
than to be intimate with Satan.

~~~

It is *better to* thank
than to grumble.

~~~

It is *better to* forgive
than to be bitter.

~~~

It is *better to* repent
than to rebel.

~~~

It is *better to* make peace
than to cause strife.

~~~

It is *better to* stand firm in faith
than to falter in fear.

~~~

It is *better to* trust and to be mobilized
than to fear and be paralyzed.

~~~

It is *better to* communicate
than to isolate.

~~~

It is *better to* be in the care of Jesus
than to be in the crosshairs of Satan.

~~~

It is *better to* be disciplined by God
than to be tempted by Satan.

~~~

It is *better to* be interceded for by the Holy Spirit
than to be accused of by the devil.

~~~

It is *better to* worship
than to worry.

~~~

It is *better to* persevere in prayer
than to pout in pity.

~~~

It is *better to* seek justice
than to plot revenge.

~~~

It is *better to* praise God
than to glorify man.

~~~

It is *better to* give sacrificially
than to horde selfishly.

~~~

It is *better to* tremble before God
than to skip with Satan.

~~~

11

It is *better to* learn through a trial
than to plead to be delivered from a trial.

~~~

It is *better to* share one another's burdens
than to add to one another's burdens.

~~~

It is *better to* delight Jesus
than to charm Satan.

~~~

It is *better to* desire things of heaven
than to dread things of earth.

~~~

It is *better to* joy in Jesus
than to laugh with Satan.

~~~

It is *better to* have perfect peace
than to expect everything to be perfect.

~~~

It is *better to* exalt God's grace
than to applaud sin's disgrace.

~~~

It is better to follow God's principles
than to chase after man's policies.

~~~

It is better to take refuge in the Lord
than to trust in man.

~~~

It is better to rectify than to justify
a wrongdoing.

~~~

It is better to rest in the Lord
than it is to fret with anxiety.

~~~

It is better to have a heart of compassion
than a mind of condemnation.

~~~

Nuggets of . . .
Wisdom

If we do not learn from our mistakes,
There is no point in making them.

~~~

Heart transformation brings
behavior modification.

~~~

If one is not a believer,
Christ's death avails nothing
for such a one.

~~~

God would not be worthy of worship if
He could be understood by man's wisdom.

~~~

Praying in Jesus' Name aligns
ourselves with His purpose.

~~~

Believers have stunned amazement
at God's salvation.

~~~

A nation is not great by man's doing,
but by God's blessing.

~~~

A proper focus on a believer's glorious future
with Christ will empower a person
to endure any kind of trouble.

~~~

You can have joy knowing that suffering is neither
meaningless nor endless.

~~~

God will not permit suffering to continue one minute
longer than necessary to fulfill
His perfect purpose for a person.

~~~

Repentance and faith in Jesus are
essential for salvation.

~~~

Jesus has the power to enter Satan's dark domain and
seize his goods and bring the believers into
His kingdom of light.

~~~

Everyone is responsible to use
what God has given him.

~~~

God uses circumstances
to teach more truth.

~~~

True faith motivates
a person to action.

~~~

Faith in the Proper Recipient of
prayer brings rewards.

~~~

If one does not know Jesus as Savior,
He will meet Him as Judge.

~~~

Being in God's will does not guarantee
easy circumstances, but it does
guarantee Jesus' presence.

~~~

Jesus brings calm into any life
when He is recognized as the
only source of help.

~~~

True worship upholds God's
worth while man's traditions
uphold the ineptitude of man.

~~~

Seeing life from God's perspective makes
possible the discernment of God's purposes.

~~~

Those who trust in riches for
salvation will be lost.

~~~

The cost of eternal life
is an undivided heart.

~~~

Those who desire glory with
God must be redeemed by Jesus
and willing to pay the price to follow Him.

~~~

Answered prayer is the fruit of faith in God.

~~~

No expression of love for
Christ is too extravagant.

~~~

To avoid yielding to temptation
demands constant vigilance.

~~~

Relationships must be built on mutual love
and respect if they are to flourish.

~~~

Perseverance and patience
in prayer are essential.

~~~

Truth is crucial to believers since a
dishonest Christian cannot hope
to stand against the father of lies.

~~~

Live today as you will wish you had lived
when you stand before God.

~~~

The smiles of heaven cannot remain on
a nation that disregards the ways of God.

~~~

For those who understand God's love,
no explanation is needed; for those
who do not understand His love,
no explanation is possible.

~~~

Perseverance is highly prized in heaven
when people wait amidst their difficulties.

~~~

Accept imperfection in yourself, and you
learn to allow for it in others.

~~~

God's disposition and kindness are founded
on strength and prompted by love.

~~~

The power of prayer is not in the one who asks, but in
the One who listens.

~~~

God would still exist apart from His creation.

~~~

God's strength has the power
of eternity behind it.

~~~

Believers are an eternal display of the
grace of God.

~~~

No sinful person has ever been granted eternal life
based on good works.

~~~

The only way a person can be justified before God
is by faith in Jesus Christ.

~~~

Glory is the visible manifestation of the sum total of
God's perfection and His attributes.

~~~

God sees all people before they are born,
and He knows who all people will become in life.

~~~

Salvation is by God's grace through faith,
apart from works.

~~~

When we love God with all our hearts,
our desires match His.

~~~

The King of kings is worshipped in the
splendor of His holiness.

~~~

The Lord rejects the half-hearted efforts of
self-satisfied Christians, but He delights in
one who repents and turns to Him.

~~~

God invites all who are weary to come to Him,
and He will give rest to all.

~~~

Nuggets of . . .
Sayings

Choices reveal what we believe about God.

~~~

Love and revenge are weights on the emotion scale –
each able to outweigh the other.

~~~

When you enter God's presence with praise, He enters
your circumstances with power.

~~~

Our worries and concerns are God's way
of reminding us to pray.

~~~

Some people reject God; others don't have time for Him. The outcome is the same.

~~~

When prayer becomes your habit,
miracles become your lifestyle.

~~~

Einstein's definition of insanity: doing the
same thing over and over, but
expecting different results.

~~~

A government that starts looking at its
own cities as the greatest threat, has itself become the
citizen's greatest threat.

~~~

God-things that may be too heavy to carry right now
pleads for you to trust God
for the results.

~~~

We know God's will by spending time
in His Word. We know God's
heart by spending time with Him.

~~~

Satan is willing to send millions of babies to heaven
to make millions of mothers and fathers murderers.

~~~

Jesus said Satan was a
murderer from the beginning.

~~~

Knowledge without love puffs up; and prayer without
faith is just a religious exercise.

~~~

We live by what God has kept secret
by trusting what He has revealed.

~~~

Sheep do not seek the shepherd;
the Shepherd seeks the sheep.

~~~

One may be a Martha in service,
but needs to be a Mary in spirit.

~~~

Safety is not found in the absence of
danger, but in the presence of God.

~~~

Since adversity draws people to the Lord,
ought not blessings do the same?

~~~

Live with what you know, and
leave the rest to God.

~~~

Contentment is an inner satisfaction
with the situation that God
has ordained for you.

~~~

Forgiveness is not earned – trust is.

~~~

Those who aim to condemn will condemn
regardless of the evidence.

~~~

The pressure of circumstance
reveals one's weakness.

~~~

A believer's burden can be
a channel of blessing.

~~~

A sinful heart must be convicted
of the need for a Savior.

~~~

Love for Christ gives courage and boldness
to do what is right in difficult situations.

~~~

Assurance of Jesus' resurrection changes
our thinking and our actions.

~~~

The once-hidden mystery of God's will
has been revealed as man's redemption.

~~~

God governed all of history to accomplish
His perfect plan of redemption at the
perfect time in history.

~~~

Christ's resurrection was the ultimate
expression of God's power.

~~~

It is never wrong to do right.

~~~

Salvation has already occurred - at the cross.

~~~

The righteous standards that man
could never attain have been
accomplished in Christ.

~~~

God's grace in Christ Jesus is to all peoples.

~~~

A believer's life should match the
excellency of Christ's calling.

~~~

The faithful stewardship of gifts on earth
will determine the position of service
in Christ's messianic reign.

~~~

Believers are called to walk
worthy of their calling.

~~~

Believers need not fear what is going on
around them - only to anticipate Jesus' return.

~~~

A whisper of deception hides
behind every temptation.

~~~

Power to a man without wisdom
is a dangerous thing.

~~~

Peace and contentment come from an
inner satisfaction with the situation
God has ordained for each of us.

~~~

No Word of God shall be void of power.

~~~

The sovereign God watches over
His words to perform them.

~~~

Justice approved the sentence;
Mercy pitied the victim.

~~~

For lack of wood, the fire
goes out, and when there is
no whisper, quarreling ceases.

~~~

Remorse without repentance avails nothing.

~~~

The guilty who have much to conceal are
often more discreet than the
innocent who have nothing to fear.

~~~

Life is the school that teaches that
all choices have consequences.

~~~

Running from God is a scary place to
be, especially with guilt, shame
and fear chasing in hot pursuit.

~~~

At times, one may struggle to match
his faith with his circumstances.

~~~

God's faithfulness is not based on the obedience of His people: rather, the enjoyment of His blessing is conditioned on their obedience to Him.

~~~

A person's past cannot dictate who he is, but it can be a part of who he will become.

~~~

Worldly remorse does not equal godly repentance.

~~~

Believers look not to escape trials – but to fulfill God's purpose in the trial.

~~~

All of Satan's apples have worms.

~~~

Sin sees the bait but is blind to the hook.

~~~

We need to know God's grace before
we can experience His peace.

~~~

Do not trust a system designed by man,
but a plan ordained by God.

~~~

Nature points us to God; Scripture
points us to the Savior.

~~~

It is not the battles and wars that made
the biggest impact in history,
but the babies who were born.

~~~

Religion is like a marriage without a spouse;
but a relationship with Jesus is complete.

~~~

Our lives are God's gift to us; what we
do with them is our gift to God.

~~~

Joy awaits us in heaven, but do not
miss the happiness of the journey.

~~~

Without trust in Jesus alone, there is
no hope for eternal life.

~~~

Those who trust God's strength
will experience His power.

~~~

Through tragedy and trials,
God grows us in ways that
easy times rarely do.

~~~

God's will for His people is to
experience their full inheritance
in Jesus Christ.

~~~

God calls His children to loyalty
as He completes His purpose.

~~~

Idols are anything we adore more than
what God created it to be.

~~~

God hears His children and
includes them in His plan.

~~~

God reigns despite human failings.

~~~

God's sovereign will mysteriously incorporates
our prayers into His replies.

~~~

Life without God is like a pencil
without lead – there is no point.

~~~

If you have a pulse, you have a purpose.

~~~

Those who forget the defenders of our
nation will themselves be forgotten.

~~~

How we view God affects how
we speak to Him and about Him.

~~~

Prayer is many things, but it is
never a waste of time.

~~~

There are no other words on earth spoken
by man that have neither more power
nor more truth than God's Word.

~~~

When darkness seems to hide His face,
we can trust in His unchanging grace.

~~~

To regard the Holy Spirit as evil is
to reject one's only hope for salvation.

~~~

Faith itself does not heal; it is the proper object of
that faith that heals.

~~~

Life is a time of learning, and making choices is
part of the process.

~~~

God reveals everything we need to know to have a
personal relationship with Him.

~~~

Do not be guilty of letting the daily wonders slip by
unnoticed. If we have our eyes down instead of up or
out, we will miss the opportunities to be amazed.

~~~

God is holy, righteous, and just,
and God is merciful, gracious, and kind with each
characteristic mingled together in
perfect harmony.

~~~

Every sinner has a future,
and every saint has a past.

~~~

Do not let the enemy pitch his tent
in your front yard.

~~~

Love is the reason we can have
confidence in our hope.

~~~

Generations come and go, yet the memories,
legacies, and lessons learned form
an integral part of each generation.

~~~

Time alone in the presence of God is a privilege
and should be a believer's priority.

~~~

The gospel of Jesus Christ does not include
good works of man.

~~~

To know God and acknowledge what He has done
is the ultimate knowledge;
to apply it to your life is wisdom.

~~~

The Holy Spirit teaches us to think with
the mind of Christ, and to pray
to the beat of His heart.

~~~

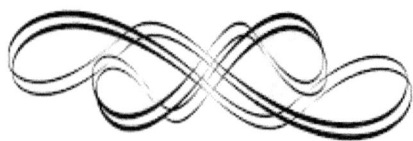

Nuggets to . . .
Ponder

Showing hospitality to a person does not require a
flashy home, but a heart to love.
Nothing more is needed.

~~~

The joy of conscious fellowship with Jesus produces a
recognizable peace and absence
of worry when faced with the challenges
and difficulties of life.

~~~

The cost of freedom determines its worth.

~~~

The difference between reckless choices and accidents is
one is choosing to put himself in harm's way; the other
is not of a person's doing.

~~~

45

Dysfunctional people are missing the gift of
life and abusing the heritage of people.

~~~

May it never be that we would throw away
our confidence for lack of patience.

~~~

How intense is the smile that is confined
to the eyes only.

~~~

The Lord God did not give Satan a chance
to confess his sins because there
would be no forgiveness for him.

~~~

God's indignation and wrath is set
ablaze because of sin; but His
unconditional love never wavers nor
is His righteousness compromised.

~~~

When the power of love overcomes the love
of power, there will be peace.

~~~

God's unimaginable plan is unfathomable
in its scope; unprecedented in its purpose; unmatched
in its wisdom; and unstoppable
in its accomplishment.

~~~

In the beginning, the Garden of Eden captivated the
essence of God's created splendor. Then sin entered,
and it became uninhabited and overgrown with weeds.
It became a symbol of man's depravity.

~~~

Those who talk with God carry through life
the price of the conversation.

~~~

If you could see your prayer life from God's perspective,
would that change the way you pray?

~~~

Anyone anywhere on earth, take notice of what God designed for a far greater complexity than our own simple wonderment.

~~~

Satan appeals to our desires for the finest in life and spurs us to choose against our understanding of truth, with tragic consequences.

~~~

The law is the minister of justice and shall never become the accomplice of injustice.

~~~

A woman's heart should be so hidden in Christ that a man should have to seek Him
first to find her.

~~~

We will never cross the ocean unless
we had courage to lose sight of the shore.

~~~

True love is acceptance of all that is,
has been, will be, and will not be.

~~~

Decisions are not nearly so hard to make if you
remember who you are and
what your values are.

~~~

The problem with prosperity preachers is that they
promise something the Bible
never intended to give us.

~~~

We can't comprehend the mysteries of God, nor can we
underestimate the power of God; He gives evidence
of both.

~~~

If trees and children are left to grow up unattended,
trees become an inextricable wilderness that nothing,
but a fire could clear, and children's lives run to
wasted ruin.

~~~

Aim to develop more confidence in God's Word
than in the opinions of others.

~~~

Wisdom is using knowledge
in a godly manner.

~~~

Contentment is not the fulfilment of what
you want, but the realization of
how much you already have.

~~~

We can only glimpse the majesty of God, but O, how
marvelous the glimpse!

~~~

If fathers master the gift of leadership, and mothers
learn the art of encouragement, shouldn't someone sit
on the curb and clap?

~~~

The Bible is meant for us to discover
what God meant it to say -
not what man wished it would say.

~~~

The Bible is the best catalog for women's
most attractive accessories.

~~~

Your mind cannot comprehend God,
but your heart can trust Him.

~~~

God's beauty, together with His holiness,
humbles the souls of humanity.

~~~

God is perfectly complete within His own being, and
yet, the whole of creation
brings Him joy.

~~~

Praying the Scriptures is bringing God's promises
into the presence of God.

~~~

There is no prayer like that which forms itself in the
words and thoughts of Scripture, since there are no
other words on earth spoken by man
that have neither more power nor more
truth than God's Word.

~~~

God shows no partiality to man, and neither should
man, which would result in
unity among men and peace with God.

~~~

To submit means to voluntarily place oneself
under the authority of another.

~~~

The enemy's lie enters our minds like
a whisper in the night.

~~~

Do not let tension, like a faceless guest, sit at your dinner table pretending not to be there.

~~~

The devil's crime was that he tempted Eve to eat that which she should not; his punishment was that he was necessitated to eat that which he would not.

~~~

Love, like the moon, illuminates in the evening of life.

~~~

A lie that is a half-truth is the blackest of lies.

~~~

Living without expectation is good. Living without hope is bad. You must not let hope turn into expectation.

~~~

One must give his want of control over to
God's control of his wants.

~~~

If obedience is the measure of our love for God, sin
must be the rebellion we hide in our hearts.

~~~

God is sovereign, and so we pray.

~~~

No matter what side of forgiveness we are on,
forgiveness gives liberty and brings healing.

~~~

The biggest troublemaker I will probably
ever have to deal with watches me from
the mirror every morning.

~~~

The world demands conformity
to their viewpoint.

~~~

Only one life, so live it well, and keep your candle
trimmed and bright. Eternity,
not time, will tell the radius
of that candle's light.

~~~

God is a God of everlasting love with immeasurable
grace and limitless mercy.

~~~

No force on earth is more effective than
the power of prayer.

~~~

Those who live by faith should expect God's discipline
to make us holy.

~~~

It is easier to tell someone of a proven fact that affects
them personally than it is to try to convince a skeptic
based on a promise that is still future.

~~~

Adding good works to the salvation message
creates a false gospel.

~~~

The power of the gospel is hinged on
two words: grace and faith.

~~~

God has taken our certificate of debt,
nailed it to the cross and stamped it
PAID IN FULL!

~~~

Nuggets of . . .
Sweet Tweets

Our small things are great to God's love;
our great things are small to God's power.

~~~

Salvation is a gift to be received;
not a goal to be achieved.

~~~

In creation, we see God's hand;
in redemption, we see His heart.

~~~

Each new day is a tangible expression
of God's grace.

~~~

God's discipline is strong encouragement to do what is right; His chastisement is His punishment for doing what is wrong.

~~~

If you pause to think, you will have
cause to thank.

~~~

Salvation is not based on our level of goodness, but on the depth of His love.

~~~

God gives evidence of His existence, but not proof since He always leaves room for faith.

~~~

Hearing the whisper of God takes practice,
and a desire to do so.

~~~

Idolatry requires no faith and gives no rewards.

~~~

Do not complain about thorns among roses;
be grateful for roses among thorns.

~~~

We teach for transformation –
not just for knowledge.

~~~

Nurturing love is loving with a purpose.

~~~

Grief never ends – it changes.
It is a passage, not a place to stay.

~~~

Grief is not a sign of weakness, nor a lack
of faith. It is the price of love.

~~~

We have given Christ Jesus countless reasons not
to love us – none of them
changed His mind.

~~~

God's love is too pure to overlook sin and too great to
abandon us; and His grace is
too precious to ignore.

~~~

Smooth seas do not make skillful sailors.

~~~

Children should see their parents on their knees
as much as they see them on the couch.

~~~

Dewdrops do God's work
as much as thunderstorms.

~~~

Little people in little places doing
little things matter to God.

~~~

Nuggets of . . .
Encouragement

Do your best to live up to
the highest you know.

~~~

The earth whispers silent reminders and
speaks bold statements of God's glory
that fills the earth. Listen to them.

~~~

Do not let your hope dim like
the flicker of a candle being
taunted by a breeze.

~~~

Stand tall in the strength of the Lord before
the enemy; bow low on bended knee in
reverence before Almighty God.

~~~

Be reminded that the Protector and Provider
has never left your side.

~~~

Marvel that God deepens our faith
beyond what could ever be imagined.

~~~

Look up! Your trust is strengthened
through every trial.

~~~

Be encouraged to know that part of heaven is
knowing God personally.

~~~

Jesus' mission was two-fold: to reveal God
to man and to reconcile man to God.
Mission accomplished! Rejoice!

~~~

Picture the Lord with His gentle hand upon you; His
fierce protection around you, and His
Holy Spirit within you, and smile.

~~~

Revel in the fact that the heavenly Father has three
objects of His love: His Son,
His church and the world.

~~~

Would you, could you, should you dare to be different?
Do not be conformed to this world but
be transformed by the renewing
of your mind.

~~~

To reach people with the gospel spoken in their own
language seems like something for which
we should be persistent in prayer.
So, soldier on, prayer warriors!

~~~

If you are in a tough season, may God help you to see it
from a perspective that encourages you.

~~~

Know that you are beloved in the Lord.

~~~

Fear not, for God is with us.
Rejoice and be glad.

~~~

It is good to know that we, who love the Lord, are
precious in His sight.

~~~

Do not lose heart. God is at work
gathering souls for eternity.

~~~

There is One who knows the way and how
to navigate through unchartered waters.
Follow Him.

~~~

Salvation was secured by the One who paid
the highest price. You have been redeemed!

~~~

Love others, and be loved, for the potential of what
we could be in the Lord.

~~~

Rejoice and be glad. You are a child of God and
an heir of salvation.

~~~

Take delight in knowing you are
God's own possession.

~~~

One day, beloved of God,
you will sing with angels.

~~~

Weeping lasts for a night,
but joy comes in the morning.

~~~

God has plans for us – to give us
a future and a hope.

~~~

The Lord is mighty in strength and
gives you abundant grace.

~~~

The Lord makes known to us the path of life;
we will know pleasures forevermore.
Anticipate the fullness of joy.

~~~

We have been given the privilege to pray to the God of the universe. Be glad to know that prayer is a haven in which to rest and a harbor from which to set sail.

~~~

It's the hard things that make us lean into Jesus. He tenderly puts His arm around your shoulders and draws you close to Himself. And your difficult time is lightened, and you feel His strength. One foot in front of the other with Jesus at your side. Be encouraged.

~~~

Let the word of Christ dwell in you richly in all wisdom. And whatever you do in word or deed, do all in the name of Lord Jesus, giving thanks to God the Father in all circumstances through Christ the Lord

~~~

Do not be discouraged. His anger is but for a moment, but His favor lasts a lifetime.

~~~

Weeping may tarry for the night, but be encouraged, joy comes in the morning.

~~~

When the righteous cry for help, the Lord hears from heaven and delivers them out of all their troubles.

~~~

The Lord is near the broken-hearted and saves the crushed in spirit.

~~~

The steadfast love of the Lord never ceases, and His mercies never end. They are new every morning.

~~~

Nuggets of . . .
Quotes

"The grace that orders our pain is the
same grace that sustains us in the darkness."
John Piper

~~~

"Pride is the national religion of hell."
David Jeremiah

~~~

"Those who trade liberty
for security have neither."
. John Adams

~~~

"I would rather laugh even when life
has other plans for me."
Dorothy Roy

~~~

"Grace is free only because the
Giver Himself has born the cost."
Philip Yancy

~~~

"We can hinder the time that should be
spent with God by remembering
we have other things to do."
Oswald Chambers

~~~

"Faith is a test of the size of your God."
Chuck Swindoll

~~~

"Advice is given so someone can accomplish something
worthwhile; news is when someone has accomplished
something of worth; good news is something someone
has accomplished of worth for you."
Jason Meyer

~~~

"G + 0 > Σ – G = God plus nothing is greater than the
sum of everything minus God." *Suzanne Lindquist*

"The Lord does not forgive excuses;
He forgives sin."
Rick Joyner

~~~

"God's Word provides stability so that we do not
capsize in the midst of the storm."
Steven Lee

~~~

"I fear the day that technology will surpass our
human interaction for that is when the world
will have a generation of idiots."
Albert Einstein

~~~

"Whatever you accomplish in life, you will have to
accomplish on your knees."
Chuck Stanley

~~~

"Waiting is the hardest part of hope."
Lewis Smedes

~~~

73

"Your eyes see your faults;
your faith sees your Savior."
Max Lucado

~~~

"You cannot make the world right, but you can
address the thigs that make you wrong."
Chuck Swindoll

~~~

"Believers are not a people of merit,
but of mercy."
Jason Meyer

~~~

"Nature is God's workshop; the sky is His resume;' and
the universe is His calling card."
Max Lucado

~~~

"If you would know the greatest sum in addition,
count your blessings."
Dorothy Roy

~~~

"I feel like someone stole my clock, and I don't know
what time it is with my life."
Bob Goris

~~~

"Love was a light that would not allow
darkness to reign in his soul."
Karen Kingsbury

~~~

"What cost God much
cannot be cheap to us."
Jason Meyer

~~~

"Praying for loved ones is a sweet duty."
C.S. Lewis

~~~

"As long as we try to defend our past or
cling to our innocence, we are still being
held hostage by prior events."
Chuck Colson

~~~

"When we recognize that our prayers must be in harmony with God's will, then this enables faith to receive the answers God gives."
Cynthia Heald

~~~

"He is no fool who gives up what he cannot keep to gain what he cannot lose."
Jim Elliott

~~~

"As for God, His way is perfect; the Word of the Lord is proven; He is a shield to all who trust in Him."
David, the Psalmist

~~~

"Watch; stand fast in the faith; be brave; be strong. Let all that you do be done with love."
Paul, New Testament writer

~~~

"Paths crossed are meant to be."
Marva Sherriff

~~~

"Just be you. You are God's idea."
Marva Sherriff

~~~

"In the beginning was the Word, and the Word was with God, and the Word was God. He was in the beginning with God. And the Word became flesh and dwelt among us."
John, New Testament gospel writer

~~~

"God delights in being involved with His children, and prayer is His gift and an invitation to intimacy with Him."
Cynthia Heald

~~~

"The next time that boy pursues you, he better do it like a dying man looking for water in the desert."
Karen Kingsbury

~~~

"As the echo of the crunching of the fruit was
still sounding in the garden,
Jesus was leaving for Calvary."
Max Lucado

~~~

"Since the will of God comes from the
heart of God, then His will is the
expression of His love."
Warren Wiersbe

~~~

"Hope is faith looking forward to the future."
R.C. Sproul

~~~

"As long as we keep our dependence on God,
He is able to take all the evils that
befall us and weave them into
His master plan."
Catherine Marshal

~~~

"A definition of faith is a conviction that God can, and a hope that He will."
Max Lucado

~~~

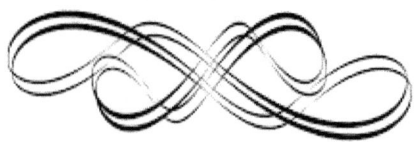

Nuggets of . . .
Blessings

May you enjoy the freshness of a new day,
the splendor of sunshine, and
the joy of the Lord.

~~~

God bless you with the peace and joy
that God displays for us in His creation.

~~~

Be filled with humble gratitude for God's
protection, His love, and His peace
poured out upon you.

~~~

May the day ahead bring you
wonderful glimpses of God's
beautiful creation all around.

~~~

May the peace and joy of the Lord
rain down on you continuously.

~~~

Man's wisdom is sometimes illogical,
but God's wisdom is always spot on.
May you be filled with godly wisdom.

~~~

May your wisdom grow, your faith made strong,
and your hope abound in God's love.

~~~

May grace and mercy be multiplied ten-fold, and may
peace and joy overflow your cup this week.

~~~

May your blessings be multiplied, and may you
recognize God's goodness in all your blessings.

~~~

Delight to know that Christ paid
for our redemption.

~~~

You are blessed. Be a blessing to others.
Give the gift of love. Abound in
every good work. Allow God to
work through you.

~~~

May you be blessed by God's extravagant love, grace,
and mercy today and always.

~~~

May you walk in the newness of life
all your years.

~~~

May the good medicine of a joyful heart overflow you
today and always.

~~~

May you be able to give thanks **in** all circumstances for this is the will of God in Christ Jesus for you.

~~~

May your thoughts dwell on whatever is true, whatever is honorable, whatever is just, whatever is pure, whatever is lovely, whatever is commendable, and whatever is worthy of praise.

~~~

May you enter His gates with thanksgiving and His courts with praise.

~~~

Nuggets of . . .

Promises

"Whoever believes in Jesus should not perish but
have everlasting life."
John 3:16, 36; 5:24

~~~

"If I go to prepare a place for you, I will come again and
receive you to Myself, that where
I am, there you may be also."
John 14:3

~~~

"Believe on the Lord Jesus Christ and you will be saved,
you and your household."
Acts 16:31

~~~

"I will never leave you nor forsake you."
Hebrews 3:5

~~~

"He who comes to Me shall never hunger, and
he who believes in Me shall never thirst."
John 6:35

~~~

"He who follows Me shall not walk in
darkness, but have the light of life."
John 8:12

~~~

"You shall know the truth and the truth
shall make you free."
John 8:32

~~~

"My sheep hear My voice, and I know them, and
they follow Me, and I give them eternal life, and
they shall never perish, neither shall anyone
snatch them out of My hand."
John 10:28

~~~

"He who loves Me will be loved by My Father, and I
will love him and manifest Myself to him."
John 14:21

"He who abides in Me, and I in him, bears much fruit;
for without Me, you can do nothing."
John 15:5

~~~

"If you abide in Me, and My words abide in you,
you will ask what you desire,
and it shall be done for you."
John 15:7, 16, 23

~~~

"Lo, I am with you always,
even to the end of the age."
Matthew 28:20

~~~

"Because you have kept My command to persevere,
I will also keep you from the hour
of trial which shall come upon the whole earth
to test those who dwell on the earth."
Revelation 3:10

~~~

"Wait on the Lord; be of good courage,
and He shall strengthen your heart."
Psalm 27:14

~~~

"The righteous cry out, and the Lord hears,
and delivers them out of all their troubles."
Psalm 34:17

~~~

"I said to you that you will die in your sins,
for if you do not believe that I am He,
you will die in your sin."
John 8:24

~~~

"I will bless you and keep you, I will make my face shine
upon you and be gracious to you, I will lift up My
countenance upon you and give you, My peace."
Numbers 6:24-26

~~~

"If the Son sets you free, you will be free indeed."
John 8:36

'There is now no condemnation for those
who are in Christ Jesus."
Romans 8:1

~~~

"God will not let you be tempted beyond what you can
bear. He will provide a way out so that
you can stand up under it."
1 Corinthians 10:13

~~~

"The peace of God which surpasses all understanding
will keep your hearts and minds in Christ Jesus."
Philippians 4:7

~~~

"This is the confidence we have in approaching God:
that if we ask anything according to
His will, He hears us."
1 John 5:14

~~~

"And this is what He promised us –
eternal life."
1 John 2:25

89

"Everyone who calls on the name of the Lord
will be saved."
Romans 10:13

~~~

Meet the Author

Rita Kroon was born in Minneapolis, but raised in St. Paul, MN. She graduated from Sibley High School and received her Liberal Arts Degree in speech/communications from Lakewood Community College.

She is an author, blogger, and Bible study leader. She has written novels, devotionals, Bible studies, wildlife magazine articles, children's short stories, poetry, and a humorous newspaper column "Rita Raps it up," and more.

Rita is a Bible study leader at her church and a participant with Bible Study Fellowship. (BSF)

Her current works are in memory of her husband, Burt, and their daughter, Rene'. She has two other daughters, 17 grandchildren, and two great grandchildren. She lives in Lexington, MN.

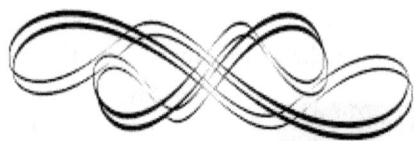

Other Books by Rita Kroon

Womanhood: Becoming a Woman of Virtue

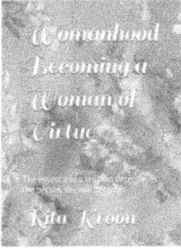

is a Bible study of eight women of the Old testament suitable for individual or group setting. It offers a 20-week in-depth section for the woman who likes to linger in the Word or an eight-week, condensed segment for the woman on the go. The in-depth section has five daily homework assignments that require approximately twenty minutes of study time per day to complete. Personal application questions are at the end of each daily lesson that are discussed in class. With the condensed section, participants gather weekly and work together on completing the weekly assignments and discussion questions in class. There is no homework!

ISBN: 9780989198554

Cancer – a Journey through the Valley is a personal memoir. Rita Kroon shares her journey through the valley where she realized her faith in God during the calm seasons of life necessitated a mighty strengthening if it was to sustain her on the battlefield of cancer.

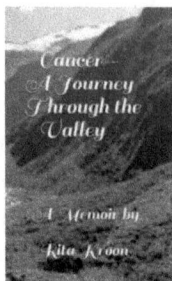

Discover how God worked such a faith while she was in the throes of cancer. Be amazed at the sovereignty of God to heal some and stand in awe to see His grace given to those for whom He has a different purpose.

ISBN: 9780989198516

Discover God through His Attributes is an

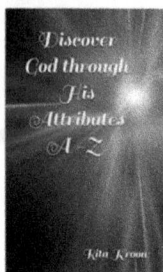

inspirational guide to help in the search for a deeper and more meaningful relationship with God. Discover who He is. Be filled with awe. Give praise to the Lord of the heavens and the earth. Reverence Him for who He is, for there is no other god or anything in the entire universe like Him. Give Him the honor due to His holy name.

ISBN: 9780989198523

Kiss Your Mommy Goodbye is a Christian novel. Mike DiSanto and his wife, Lisa, are sinking in quicksand. Their four-year marriage ends in a courtroom, with full custody of their two-year old daughter, Maddy, awarded to Lisa. Mike is devastated, but Lisa stands tall like a princess, though she lost her kingdom.

In his desperate quest to provide love and stability as a part-time father to Maddy, Mike does the unthinkable. He took a risk and lost. Mike learns that every choice has consequences as he struggles to reconcile and rebuild broken relationships. It is a story of hope, forgiveness, and peace with God and one another.

ISBN: 9780989198561

40 Days of Assurance is a daily devotional with selected Scripture verses, the obstacles that challenge, and how to overcome those challenges through personal application of the principles presented. Drink deeply from God's word, and rest in its assurance.

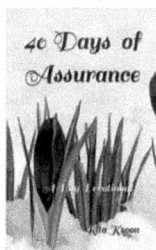

ISBN: 9780989198530

40 Days of Encouragement is a daily devotional which includes a goal for each selection with those obstacles that may intrude, and how to overcome the roadblocks through personal application of the principles presented.

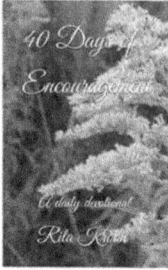

Drink deeply from God's word and be encouraged.

ISBN: 9780989198547

40 Days in the Wilderness is a daily devotional that includes a goal for each selection with the hindrances that may interrupt, and how to overcome the barricades through personal application of the principles presented. Drink deeply from God's word and be refreshed.

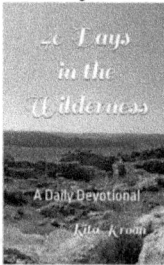

ISBN: 9780989198509

Praying the Scriptures is a collection of prayers and promises taken from God's Word, since no Word of God shall be void of power. When words cannot be found to say what is on your heart, this collection of prayers is meant to guide you through those moments of solitude. At other times when words to express your joy through praise and worship seem elusive, you can turn to the Scriptures.

Rita Kroon

If praying may be unfamiliar, or has long ago been abandoned, Praying the Scriptures is one way to begin afresh. Discover the joy and power of prayer, and revel in the surety of His promises. Let the Lord lead you in the pursuit of His righteousness so that you may know the joy of Praying the Scriptures and trusting in His promises.

ISBN: 9780989198585

Letters from the Past is historical fiction. Through personal letters, eight women of Biblical times reveal the emotional impact of rape, infertility, incest, betrayal, and family dysfunction. They write of their trials and victories to the women of the twenty-first century. They also share their joy in overcoming seemingly impossible situations. One young woman risks her life when she is called to lead a nation. She responds with the brave words, "If I perish, I perish.

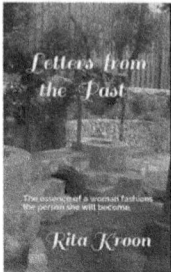

"Trial turns to triumph when the thread of God's faithfulness is traced through these authentic women from ancient times to today's woman. Suddenly there is no distance in time, no generational gap, and no heart left unturned. Today's woman will be challenged, filled with hope, and encouraged through the personal letters from Eve, Sarah, Rebekah, Rachel, Miriam, Deborah, Tamar, and Esther. She will celebrate accomplishments of ordinary women in extraordinary circumstances.

ISBN: 9780989198578

More Nuggets from My Pocket is a collection of sayings, wit, insights, quotes, wisdom, promises, prayer, and more that were gathered where the trail led to an open meadow.

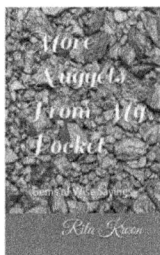

These gems will inspire you and encourage you no matter what path of life you travel. Stop to ponder the insights given, or to discover a fresh perspective, or to glean new meaning to old sayings.

More Nuggets from My Pocket is my way of giving you such an opportunity to explore rather than to merely hurry on your way. You may even want to share a nugget with a friend to encourage.

ISBN: 9798682187225

Extra Nuggets from My Pocket is a collection of sayings meant to stir your imagination, fill your heart, and satisfy your desire for fresh "Ah, moments."

When the path of life leads me beside still waters, I search the beach for Extra Nuggets like one does when looking for agates on the North Shore. Many of these gems of truth, wit, quotes, prayers, blessings, and more are mine and others are those I gathered along the way and tucked into my pocket.

Come, walk with me along the beach and discover your Extra Nuggets from Your Pocket to share with a friend.

ISBN: 9798587330566

Almost-Forgotten Nuggets is a collection of truthful, inspiring, and wise sayings, and follows the footprints of its three siblings, ***Nuggets from My Pocket, More Nuggets from My Pocket,*** **and** ***Extra Nuggets from My Pocket.*** The path is familiar, but the landscape has an added dimension of newness that makes the pleasant journey a most memorable one.

Almost-Forgotten Nuggets is sure to take you on an adventure much like a treasure hunt where one seeks the next gem to keep for your pocket or to share with a friend along the way.

Here is a preview of what is inside: "Unconfessed sin is like a math problem: it divides the heart; adds woes; subtracts peace and multiplies consequences."

ISBN: 9798511772042

John ~ A Mini Study is an interactive Bible study of the Gospel of John and is suitable for individual and group setting. It uses a loosely structured <u>Observation</u>, <u>Interpretation</u>, and <u>Application</u> method of study with summarizing <u>Principles</u> in an easy-to-read format. One way to think of it like this: The <u>*observation of facts*</u> is like reading a menu. The <u>*interpretation*</u> is looking at the number of calories or the price on the menu. The <u>*application questions*</u> are the main course – the most satisfying part of the meal that energizes us for action. The <u>*principle*</u> is the appetizer that sharpens our desire for what is coming next. <u>*Something to ponder*</u> is the dessert and like most desserts, is just an occasional treat.

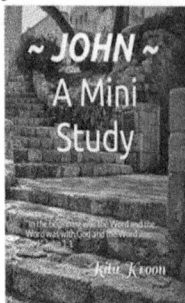

We learn what we can, apply what we know, and leave the rest to **God** is the <u>*gratuity*</u> we leave for the one who gave us dinner out ~ John, the disciple whom Jesus loved.

If we set a goal to connect with God and His truth every time we study His Word, we allow Him to mature us in our walk of faith.

"This is the disciple who testifies of these things and wrote these things, and we know this testimony is true." John 21:24 "BEHOLD! The Lamb of God!"

ISBN: 9798545633234

Pebbles of Truth is a collection of short, timeless sayings of truth that are filled with wisdom, give great insight, plus unforgettable quotes, encouragement, blessings, thoughts to remember, and explore God's greatness. These pebbles of truth connect the heart with one's imagination the same way pebbles on a beach connect the water and the land.

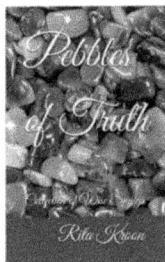

Here's a sneak peek: "Learn to write your hurts in the sand and to carve your blessings in stone." Here's another: "Man contributed nothing to his salvation except the sin that made it necessary."

Pebbles of Truth is sure to give you a delightful reading and sharing experience.

ISBN: 9798842917037

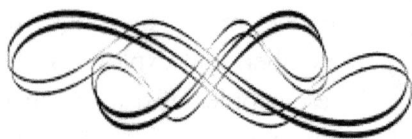

A Walk to the Well –
A place where women can find
encouragement, hope and inspiration
through blog posts and books

awalktothewell.com